LIBRETTO OF

MEFISTOFELE

Opera in Four Acts

LIBRETTO OF

MEFISTOFELE

Opera in Four Acts

By

ARRIGO BOITO

TRANSLATED AND ADAPTED BY

THEODORE T. BARKER

ISBN: 978-93-5128-839-8(HB)

First Published in 1908
Indian Reprint in 2017

Published by

Kalpaz Publications
C-30, Satyawati Nagar,
Delhi – 110052
E-mail: kalpaz@hotmail.com
Website: kalpazpublications.com
Ph.: +91-9212142040

Cataloging in Publication Data—DK
Courtesy: D.K. Agencies (P) Ltd. <docinfo@dkagencies.com>

Boito, Arrigo, 1842-1918, **author.**
Libretto of Mefistofele : opera in four acts / by Arrigo Boito ; translated and adapted by Theodore T. Barker.
pages cm
Italian text with parallel translation in English.
"First published in 1908"—Title page verso.
ISBN 9789351288398

1. Faust, -approximately 1540—Drama. 2. Operas—Librettos. I. Barker, Theodore T., translator,, editor. II. Boito, Arrigo, 1842-1918. Mefistofele. Libretto. III. Boito, Arrigo, 1842-1918. Mefistofele. Libretto. English. IV. Title. V. Title: Mefistofele.

ML50.B686M32 2017 DDC 782.10268 23

DRAMATIS PERSONÆ.

MEFISTOFELES	*Bass.*	WAGNER	*Tenor*
FAUST	*Tenor.*	HELEN	*Soprano.*
MARGARET	*Soprano.*	PANTALIS	*Contralto.*
MARTHA	*Contralto.*	NEREUS	*Tenor.*

Celestial Phalanxes, Mystic Choir. Cherubs (Boys), Penitents, Wayfarers, Men-at-arms, Huntsmen, Students, Citizens, Populace, Townsmen, Witches, Wizards, Greek Chorus, Sirens, Naiads, Greek Dancers, Warriors.

ARGUMENT.

THE Prologue opens in the nebulous regions of space, in which float the invisible legions of angels, Cherubs and seraphs, that, uniting with the celestial trumpets, lift their voices in a hymn of praise to the Supreme ruler of the universe. Mefistofele enters on the scene at the close of the anthem, and standing erect amid the clouds, with his feet upon the border of his cloak, mockingly addresses the Deity. In answer to the question from the Mystic Choir, "Knowest thou Faust?" he answers contemptuously, and offers a wager that he will entice him to evil, and thus gain a victory over the powers of Good. The wager is accepted, and the Spirits resume their chorus of praise.

ACT I — The drama opens on Easter Sunday, at Frankfort-on-the-main. Crowds of people of all conditions move in and out the City gates. Among them appears a grey Friar, an object of both reverence and dread to those near him. The aged Dr. Faust and his pupil Wagner descend from a height and enter upon the scene, followed by the Friar, whose movements they discuss. Faust returns to his laboratory, still followed by the friar, who unheeded, enters with him, and conceals himself in an alcove. Faust gives himself to meditation, and upon opening the sacred volume, is startled by a shriek from the Friar as he rushes from his place of concealment. Faust makes the all-potent "sign of Solomon," when Mefistofele throws off his disguise, — and in his own person appears in the garb of a knight, with a black cloak upon his arm. In reply to Faust's questionings, he declares himself the spirit that denieth all things, desiring only the complete ruin of the world, and a return to chaos and night. He offers to make Faust the companion of his wanderings, upon certain conditions, to which the latter agrees, saying: "If thou wilt bring me one hour of peace, in which my soul may rest — if thou wilt unveil the world and myself before me -- if I may find cause to say to some flying moment, 'Stay, for thou art blissful,' then let me die, and let Hell's depths engulf me." The contract completed, Mefistofele spreads his cloak, and both disappear through the air.

ACT II., opens with the garden scene. Faust (rejuvenated, and under the name of Henry.) Margaret, Mefistofele and Martha stroll here and there in couples, chatting and love-making. Thence Mefistofele takes Faust to the heights of the Brocken, where he witnesses the orgies of the Witches' Sabbath. The Fiend is welcomed and saluted as their King. Faust, benumbed and stupified, gazes into the murky sky, and beholds there a vision of Margaret, pale, sad, and fettered with chains.

ACT III.—The scene is a prison. Margaret lies extended upon a heap of straw, mentally wandering, and singing to herself; Mef. and Faust appear outside the grating. They converse hurriedly, and Faust begs for the life of Margaret. Mefistofele promises to do what he can, and bids him haste, for the infernal steeds are ready for flight. He opens the cell, and Faust enters it. Margaret think the jailors have come to release her, but at length recognizes her lover. She describes what followed his desertion of her, and begs him to lay her in death beside her loved ones. Faust entreats her to fly with him, and she finally consents, saying, that in some far distant isle they may yet be happy The voice of Mefistofele in the background recalls her to the reality of the situation. She shrinks away from Faust, prays to Heaven for mercy, and dies, while the voices of the celestial choir are heard singing softly "She's saved!" Faust and Mefistofele escape, as the executioner and his escort appear in the background.

In Act IV., Mefistofele takes Faust to the shores of the Peneus, in the vale of Tempe, when they agree to separate for a while, each seeking his fortune on a different path. Faust is ravished with the beauty of the scene, while Mefistofele finds that the orgies of the Brocken were more to his taste.

'Tis the night of the classic Sabbath. A band of young maidens appear, singing and dancing. Mefistofele, annoyed and confused, retires. Helen enters with Chorus, and absorbed by a terrible vision, rehearses the story of Troy's destruction. Faust enters, richly clad in the costume of a knight of the fifteenth century, followed by Mefistofele, Nereus, Pantalis, and others, with little fauns and sirens, and kneeling before Helen, addresses her as his ideal of beauty and purity. Thus pledging to each other their love and devotion, they wander through the bowers and are lost to sight.

In the Epilogue, we find Faust in his laboratory once more — an old man, with death fast approaching, mourning over his past life, with the holy volume open before him. Fearing that Faust may yet escape him, Mefistofele spreads his cloak, and urges Faust to fly with him through the air. Appealing to Heaven, Faust is strengthened by the sound of angelic songs, and resists. Foiled in his effort, Mefistofele conjures up a vision of beautiful sirens. Faust hesitates a moment, flies to the sacred volume, and cries, "Here at last I find salvation." Then falling on his knees in prayer, effectually overcomes the temptations of the Evil one. He then dies amid a shower of rose-leaves, and to the triumphant song of a celestial choir. Mefistofele has lost his wager, and holy influences have prevailed.

J. FRANK GILES, Music Printer, Boston.

MEFISTOFELE.

BY

ARRIGO BOITO.

PROLOGUE IN HEAVEN.

Knowest thou FAUST?—*Goethe, Prologue in Heaven.*

Clouds. The sounding of the seven trumpets. The seven tones. The celestial phalanxes behind the clouds, invisible. Mystic chorus, Cherubs, Penitents, afterwards* MEFISTOFELE *alone in the shadows.

CORO.

Ave! Signor degli angeli e dei santi!
Ave! Signor degli angeli e dei santi!
Ave! Signor, Signor degli angeli!
O Signor, Signor degli angeli!
E dei volanti, e dei volanti, cherubini d'or!
Ave! Ave! Signor!
Dall' eterna armonia del l'Universo,
Nel glauco, spazio immerso,
Immerso emana un verso di supremo amor
Di supremo amor, e s'erge a te
Per l'aure uzzurre e cave in suon soave.
Ave! Ave! Ave! Ave!

CHORUS.

Hail! Sov'reign Lord of saints and angels holy;
Hail! mighty Lord of the angelic hosts!
Sov'reign Lord of all the heavenly hosts,
Of the seraphs, e'er bending lowly,
And of the cherubs with their wings of gold!
Hail! Lord of cherubs, with their wings of gold.
From the harmonies eternal of space unbounded,
From azure regions unsounded.
Ascends a joyful anthem of supremest love—
Joyful anthem of love—up to the throne.
Through azure depths unbounded,
Anthems are sounded.
Hail! all hail, all hail, hail to thee!

(Trumpets within the clouds.)

MEFISTOFELE.

Ave, Signor!
Perdona si il mio gergo,
Si lascia un po'da tergo,
Le superne teodie del paradiso;
Perdona si il mio viso non porta il raggio
Che inghirlanda i crini degli alti cherubini;
Perdona se dicendo, io corro rischio
Di buscar qualche fischio.
Il Dio piccin della piccina terra
Ognor traligna ed erra.
E, al pardi grillo saltellante, a caso,
Spinge fra gli a stri il naso;
Poi con tenace fatuità superba
Fa il suo trillo nell' erba.
Boriosa polve tracotato atómo!
Fantasima dell' umo! E tale il fa
Quell' ebra illusione
Ch' egli chiama Ragion, Ragion.
Ah! Si Maestro divino,
In bujo fondo crolla il padron del mondo,
E non mi dà più il cuor, tant' è fiaccato,
Di tentarlo al mal.

MEFISTOFELE. *(With his feet upon the border of his cloak.)*

Hail! Sov'reign lord!
Forgive me, if my bawling
Somewhat behind is falling
Those sublime anthems, sung in heavenly places.
Forgive me, if my face is now wanting the radiance
That, as with a garland, the cherub legion graces;
Forgive me, if in speaking, some risk I'm taking
Of irreverent outbreaking!
The puny king of puny earth's dominions,
Erreth thro' wrong opinions;
And like a cricket, with a long leap rushing,
'Mid stars his nose is pushing;
Then, with superb fatuity tenacious,
Thrills with pride contumacious!
Vainglorious atom! proud 'mid dire confusion,
Phantom of man's delusion!
And, with like shams, puts he forth the mad illusion.
He reason names as right! All right!
Ah! In such deep degradation
Is fallen the master, lord of the whole creation,
No more have the will, while in that station,
Him to tempt to ill!

CORO.

Tè noto Faust?

MEFISTOFELE.

Il più bizzarro pazzo ch' io mi conosca,
In curiosa forma ei ti serve da senno.
Inassopita bramosia di saper
Il fa tapino ed anelante;
Egli vorrebbe quasi trasumanar
E nulla scienza al cupo suo delirio è confine.
Io mi sobbarco ad aescarlo per modo
Ch' ei si trovi nelle mie reti;
Vuoi tu farne scommessa?

CORO.

E sia.

MEFISTOFELES.

Sia! vecchio Padre, a un rude gioco t' avventurasti.
Ei morderà nel dolce pomo de' vizi.
E sovra il Re del ciel.
Avrò vittoria!

CORO.

Sanctus! Sanctus! Sanctus!

MEFISTOFELE.

(Di tratto in tratto m' è piacevol cosa vedere il
Vecchio e dal guastarmi seco molto mi guardo;
E bello udir l'eterno
Col Diavolo parlar sì umanamente.)

CORO.

Siam nimbi volanti dai limbi,
Nei santi splendori vaganti
Siam coridi bimbi d' amori,
Siam nimbi volanti dai limbi,
Nei santi splendori, ecc., ecc., ecc.

MEFISTOFELE.

E lo sciame legger degli angioletti;
Come dell' api n' ho ribrezzo e noja.

CORO.

Un giorno nel fango mortale,
Perdemmo il tripudio dell' ale,
L' aureola di luce e di fiori;
Ma sciolti dal lugubre bando,
Pregando contando, danzando,
Noi Torniamo fra gli angioli ancor.
La danza in angelica spira
Si gira, si gira, si gira.
La danza in angelica spira, ecc., ecc., ecc.
Fratelli, te niamci per mano,
Fin l' ultimo cielo lontano
Noi sempre dobbiamo danzar;
Fratelli, le morbide penne
Non cessino il volo perenne
Che intorno al Santissimo Altar.
Fratelli, te niamci per mano, ecc., ecc., ecc.
La danza in angelica spira
Si gira, si gira, si gira, ecc., ecc., ecc.
Siam nimbi volanti dai limbi,
Nei santi splendori vaganti,
Siam coridi bimbi, d' amori,
Siam nimbi volanti dai limbi, ecc., ecc., ecc.

MYSTIC CHORUS. (*Within.*)

Thou knowest Faust?

MEFISTOFELES.

Maddest of all madmen of my acquaintance,
In many curious ways doth he faithfully serve you.
'Tis his unquenchable desire, all to know,
That keeps him always panting and breathless;
To rise above his race he e'er doth aspire;
Nothing in science or learning bounds his craving for all-wisdom!
Yet I'll engage in such a way to entice him,
That ensnared you shortly will find him.
Wilt make me a wager?

MYSTIC CHORUS.

Agreed!

MEFISTOFELES.

So! Powers immortal, 'tis on a hazardous game you venture!
Let him but taste the sweet fruits that vice doth [offer,
And o'er the powers of good
I'll be victorious!

CHORUS.

Holy! Holy! Holy!

MEFISTOFELES.

(From time to time, it is delightful to converse with the rulers,
And I take good care with them ne'er to quarrel;
'Tis pleasant also to hear thus
The powers of good and ill freely conversing.)

CHORUS OF BOYS. (*Within.*)

We're spirits from limbo upsoaring,
The regions celestial exploring;
We're choirs of fair cherubs adoring,
We're spirits from limbo upsoaring,
The regions celestial exploring, etc., etc. etc.

MEFISTOFELES.

'Tis the soft droning hum of winged cherubs;
Like bees I hold them in great detestation.
[*Disappears.*

CHORUS OF BOYS. (*Within.*)

One day, in earth's miry dominions,
We lost the free play of our pinions.
Our aureoles, flaming and radiant;
But out from sin's shadows advancing,
Thro' praying and singing and dancing,
We now soar with the angels once more.
The spirals angelic we're learning,
And turning, and turning, and turning,
The spirals angelic we're learning, etc., etc.
Now, brothers, unite we our legions,
And upwards to heaven's high regions
We e'er must soar our spiral flight;
And, brothers, our wings, soft and tender,
Shall cease not their service to render,
Till at heaven's altars we a light.
Now, brothers, unite we our legions, etc., etc.
The spiral angelic we're learning,
And turning, and turning, and turning, etc.
We're spirits from limbo upsoaring,
The regions celestial exploring;
We're choirs of fair cherubs, adoring, etc., etc.

SALMODIA FINALE.

CORO. (*Insieme.*) LE PEN. (*Della terra.*)

Salve Regina! s' innalzi un eco,
Dal mondo cieco, dal mondo cieco
Alla divina reggia dei ciel.
Col nostro canto, col nostro pianto,
Domiam l' intenso foco del senso,
Col nostro canto, mite e fedel.
Odi la pia, la pia prece serena.

CORO. (*Insieme.*)

Sugli astri, sui venti, sui mondi,
Sui limpidi azzurri profondi,
Sui raggi del sol.
La danza in angelica spira,
Si gira, si gira, si gira, si gira, ecc., ecc.

LE PEN.

Ave Maria! gratia plena.

CORO. (*Insieme.*)

La danza in angelica spira,
Si gara, si gara, si gara, ecc., ecc.

LE PEN.

Ave Maria, gratia plena.

CORO. (*Insieme.*)

La danza in angelica spira,
Si gira, si gira, si gira, ecc., ecc.

LE PEN.

Odi lapia prece serena!
Ave Maria! gratia plena!
Il pentimento lagrime spande.
Di queste blande turbe il la mento
Accolga il cielo, accolga il ciel!
Odi lapia, lapia prece serena, etc., etc. etc.

CORO.

Oriam, oriam per quei morienti,
Per quei morienti, ecc, ecc., ecc.
Ave, Ave, Ave, ecc.

TUTTI.

Ave Signor! degli angeli e
Dei santi e delle sfere erranti,
E dei volanti e, dei volanti cherubini d'ör, ecc.
Dall' eterna armonia dell' Universo,
Nel glauco spazio immerso
Emana un verso d' supremo amor.
E s' erge a Te per l' aure azzure e cave
In suon soave, Ave! Ave!

FINE DEL PROLOGO.

PSALMODIC FINALE.

CHORUS. (*Within.*) PENITENTS. (*From the earth.*)

Hail Queen of heaven! an echo arises.
Earth-born in sorrow, craving to borrow
Aid from the heavenly regions of joy.
With watch unsleeping, with prayers and weeping.
Help us! engaging 'gainst passions' raging,
While grateful songs our tongues shall employ.
Hear thou the prayers to thy throne now ascending!

CHORUS. (*Within.*)

O'er planets, on whirwinds, our legions
Thro' blue depths of space's far regions,
O'er rays of bright suns.
The dances angelic we're learning,
And turning, and turning, and turning, &c.

PENITENTS.

Ave Maria! full of compassion!

CHORUS. (*Within.*)

The spiral angelic we're learning,
And turning, and turning, and turning, etc.

PENITENTS.

Ave Maria! full of compassion!

CHORUS. (*Within.*)

The dances angelic we're learning,
And turning, and turning, and turning, etc.

PENITENTS.

Hear thou the prayers to heaven ascending!
Ave Maria! full of compassion!
Tears of repentance they freely are shedding.
Let their complaints, thro' thy love wide-spreading,
Find acceptation with thee in heaven!
Hear thou the pray'rs that to heav'n are ascending!

CHORUS.

We pray thee for the dying,
For these dying. etc., etc. etc.
Ave, Ave, Ave, etc.

ALL.

Hail, sov'reign Lord of angel hosts,
And ruler of the spheres ever-moving, [gold!
Of seraph legions and of cherubs with their wings of
From the hormonies eternal of space unbounded.
From azure regions unsounded,
Raises an anthem of supremest love,
Up to thy throne, thro' azure depths unbounded,
Anthems are sounded. Hail, all hail, thee!

END OF PROLOGUE.

ATTO PRIMO. ACT FIRST.

LA DOMENICA DI PASQUA. (EASTER SUNDAY.)

Should there come a time when I can say to the flying moment, "Stay, thou art blissful," then let me die.—GOETHE. *(In* FAUST'S *Laboratory.)*

SCENE.—*Frankfort-on-the Maine. Gates and bastions. People of all conditions leaving the city in groups. Noise and murmur of the crowd. Holiday bells. Later* FAUST *and* WAGNER.

(Tre Studenti, quattro Borghesi, Due Cacciatore, Divisi in due gruppi.)

CORO.

Perchè di la?
—Volgiamo verso il casin di caccia.
—E noi verso il mulino.

(Otto Fanciulle, traversano la scena contando.)

Del vago April la traccia,
Brilla e ride d'intorno
Baldezza e leggiadria. [*Passano.*

CORO.

Che fate compari?
—Stiam colla compagnia.
—Messeri, andiamo a Burgdorf, Costà son le più buffe mattie!
La miglior birra, le donne e le baruffe più dilettose.
—Pazzi! pazzi! Vi prude ancor la schiena?

(Due banditore con una scritta in mano e a suon di tromba attrae la folla dei passeggiatori; sta con lui un araldo. Della parte opposta un cerrentano seguito da Hanswurst. La passeggiata diventa sempre piu vivace. Un gruppo di balestrieri e popolani, avvicinandosi ad un rivenditore di birra.

CORO.

—Qua un bicchiere!
—Vogliam bere!
—E fare un drindisi
—Ai folli amor!
—E alla beltà corriva!
—Evviva! Be viam, ri daimo, cantiamo!

(Un frate grigio col cappuccio sul volto cammina tra la folla, alcuni lo inchinano, altri lo sfuggono. Passa.

CORO. *(Traendo verso un lato della scena)*

Guarda la! Quanti focosi destrier,
Quanti focosi destrieri scalpitan! la
C' è il buffon, c' è il buffon!
C' è il falconier, c' è il buffon!
Rendiam o maggio al Prence! O maggio al prence!
Largo, largo al suo passaggio!
Che abbarbaglio di gualdane!
Che frastuno di campane!
Gloria al principe!
Vien la folla a onde a onde

(Three Students, four townspeople, two huntsmen divided into groups.)

CHORUS.

Why go ye there
We're going to our hunting-cabin.
And we go towards the miller's.

(Eight Girls pass singing.

Of April fair the traces,
Smiling appear in all places
Declaring spring is here. [*Exeunt.*

CHORUS.

What do you here my comrades?
As do the others near.
Sirs, let us go to to Burgdorf,
The maddest of all jokers are there!
Beer there the best is,
The ladies and the brawlings are most delightful!
Madcaps! Madcaps! to be there now you're longing.

(Two Criers, with a proclamation, draw together the crowds by the sound of a trumpet, a Herald is near. On the other side, a charlatan from Hanswurst. The crowd getting lively. A group of halberdiers and peasants surround a seller of beer,)

CHORUS.

Here, some beer!
Quick, some beer!
And let us have a song
To mirth and love—
To love and beauty singing!
Hurrah, then! for laughing, singing, and quaffing!

(A grey Friar, with his hood over his face, wanders among the crowd. Some kneel to him, others shun him. The crowd, pointing to a side of the scene.)

CHORUS.

Look there! gay cavaliers now appear,
Gay cavaliers now appear tramping everywhere.
There's the fool! there's the fool!
Here comes the falconer too!
Now to the prince homage render—
Hail to the prince, our defender!
Room there, for the prince's passage!
What a troop of soldiers dashing!
How the bells are loudly crashing!
Now the crowd comes onward rushing,

CORO.

S'arrabatta, si confonde—
Largo, largo! Guarda la! Ah!

(La cavalcata passa. Alla sua testa il Principe elettore, Dame, Dignitari, Paggi, il buffone, il falconiere, ecc. Molti passeggiatori seguono curiosamente la cavalcata.)

CORO.

Quanti focosi destrier!
Quanti bei cavalier!
I focosi destrieri! scalpitan là!
Fate omaggio al Principe,
Fate omaggio, omaggio, al Prence! Ah!

(FAUST e WAGNER discendono da un' altura.)

FAUST. *(Recit.)*

Al soave raggiar di primavera
Si scoscendono i ghiacci e già rinverda
Di speranza la valle;
Il vecchio inverno fugge al monte
E il sol rallegra e avviva forme e color;
Se peranco al piano non isbucciano i fior,
La somma luce fa pullulare in cambio i bei borghesi
Azzimati di festa.

(Entra in scena rumorosamente una frotta di popolani e popolane.)

WAGNER. *(Recit.)*

Movere a diporto con voi,
Dottor, è onorevole e saggio;
Pur da me solo,
Qui mi schiferei fra questa gente,
M' è di noja il vulgo.

(FAUST e WAGNER si ritirano nel fondo.)

CORO.

Juhé! Juhé! Juhiesa! heisa! hé! Ah! hé!
Il bel giovanetto sen viene alla festa,
Coi nastri al farsetto, coi fior sulla testa.
E sotto ad un pioppo fanciulle e compar
Si danno a danzar un matto galoppo.

(Incominciano a danzare l' Obertas.)

Juhé! Tutti vanno alla rinfusa,
Sulla musica confusa. Ah! tra, la, la, ecc.
Alla rinfusa tutti van, danziamo,
Alla rinfusa tutti van cantiamo,
La danza scalpita sul suol,
La danza rotonda
Tutti vanno alla rinfusa. Juhè, juhè, ecc.
Sorri don le donne al bel torneamento,
Svolazzan le gonne portate dal vento;
E il bruno e la bionda son stretti in un vol,
E scalpita al suol la danza rotonda, ecc.
E sotto ad un pioppo fanciulle e compar,
Si danno a danzare, un matto galoppo, ecc.
Si danno a danzar, a danzar, a danzar, ecc.

(Le danze cessano. Il giorno s'oscura lentamente e la scena va spopolandosi a poco a poco.)

FAUST *(a WAGNER.)*

Sediam sovra quel sasso.
Osserva come fulgoreggian a vespro le capanne.
Declina il giorno.

CHORUS.

Scolding fighting, pulling pushing—
Room there—room there! Look ye there! Ah!

(The cavalcade passes. At its head come the Prince Elector, Ladies, Dignitaries, Pages, the falconer, the the fool, etc. Many persons join in the cavalcade.)

CHORUS.

What fiery steeds now appear!
And what gay cavaliers!
Gallant horsemen are there, trampling everywhere;
Our respect for the prince we will show,
And our homage bestow in his honor. Ah!

(Dispersing. FAUST and WAGNER descend from a height.)

FAUST. *(Recit.)*

'Neath the warm, sunny beams of early springtime
Ice and snow quickly vanish,
And verdure bright and gay,
With hope cheers the valley.
Winter to mountain tops is fleeing,
The genial sun restoreth colors and forms;
If as yet the pra'ries have not put forth their flow'rs.
The higher places put forth instead
Their numbers of happy peasants,
Clad in festival garments.

(A crowd of people enter, noisily.)

WAGNER. *(Recit.)*

Roving thus at pleaure, with you, sir,
Brings us both wisdom and honor;
But, for my own part,
I would fain avoid this crowd of people,
Which to me is distasteful.

(FAUST and WAGNER retire to the background.)

CHORUS.

Juhé! Juhé! Juheisa! heisa! hé! Ah! hé!
The handsome young fellows have come to the dancing,
With hats trim'd with gay flow'rs and with ribbons they're prancing
And under the poplars, with matron or maid,
They dance in the shade a mad gallopade!

(They begin to dance the Obertas.)

Juhé! All is going to dire confusion,
With the music in collusion. Ah, ah, ah! Tra, la, la, etc.
Ah, yes, 'mid dire confusion goes our dancing!
And with a false collusion flows our singing;
Dancing, we stamp upon the ground, etc.
The merry-go-round—Ah!
All is going to confusion. Juhé, Juhé etc.
The ladies are laughing as madly they're turning,
Their gowns whirl around them, their faces are burning;
The darkest and fairest are whirling around, etc.
And trip o'er the ground, still whirling and whirling,
And under the poplars, both young men and maids,
Give all up to dancing, their mad gallopades, etc.
As swift they go round, gaily they dance, etc.

(The dance ends. Chorus and dancers departing. Day slowly darkens.)

RECIT. FAUST *(to WAGNER.)*

Now let us here be seated.
Observe how brightly evening's rays
Touch the mountains and the cabins.
Day is declining.

WAGNER.

E l'ora degli spettri; essi sen vanno fra i vapor della serra
Ordendo reti sotto i piedi dell' uom.
Andiam; s'impregna l'orizzonte di nebbia,

CORO.

Ah!

WAGNER.

A notte bruna torna dolce la casa.
A che sogguardi, nel crepuscolo assorto immobil- [mente.

(Ritorna il frate grigio e si dirige lento e spettrale alla volta di FAUST.)

FAUST.

Vedi quel frate grigio in mezzo i campi
Vagolante laggiù?

WAGNER.

Da lungo tratto, maestro, l'avvisai;
Nulla di strano appare in esso.

FAUST.

Aguzza ben lo sguardo.
Per chi tieni quel frate?

WAGNER.

E un questüante che va alla cerca.

FAUST.

Lo contempla.
Ei move in tortuose spire
E s'avvicina lento alla nostra volta.
Oh! se non erro, or me di foco imprime al suol!

WAGNER.

Ah, no! fantasima quest' è del tuo cervello,
Io non iscorgo che un frate grigio,
Timidamente va per la sua via;

FAUST.

Par vada filando de' lacci intorno a noi.

WAGNER.

Due sconosciuti noi siam per esso.
Ah! fantasima quest' è del tuo
Cervello, del tuo cervel.

FAUST. *(Con ribrezzo.)*

La spira si tringe, ei n' è vicin. Ah!

WAGNER. *(Freddamente.)*

L'osserva: è un frate grigio,
Non è uno spettro;
Brontola orazioni rigirando un rosario.
Andiam, maestro.

[*Il frate li segue.*

SOPRANI CORO.

Il bel giovinetto
Sen viene alla festa.
Il bruno e la bionda
Son stretti in un vol.

TENROI CORO.

Ah!

[*Canti lontani.*

(Mutamento di scena.)

WAGNER.

This is the hour of phantoms, when they glide
Among the vapors of evening,
Laying snares to trap the footsteps of men.
Let's go; with mists the pale horizon is shadow'd.

CHORUS. *(Within, and distant.)*

Ah!

WAGNER.

At nightfall, tho't doth always turn to one's dwelling.
What are you watching, thus absorbed—
In the twilight, still as a statue?

(The grey friar returns spectrally towards FAUST.)

FAUST.

See you? 'Tis that grey friar, amid the meadows,
Wandering slow, to and fro.

WAGNER.

For many minutes I've noticed his approach;
But nothing strange I find about him.

FAUST.

Most carefully observe him.
For whom take you that friar?

WAGNER.

He is a beggar now making his circuit.

FAUST.

Watch him closely!
In tortuous circles he is moving,
And thus approaches slowly within our vision.
Oh, if I err not, on the ground his tracks are flame!

WAGNER.

Ah, no! 'tis but some passing fancy in your brain revolving;
I nought can see there but some grey friar
Timidly going on his homeward way.

FAUST.

To my mind, he's laying some snares around us here.

WAGNER.

We for him are two unknown men only,
Ah! 'tis only passing fancy in your brain,
Revolving within your brain.

FAUST. *(With a shudder.)*

The circuit is closing, and he is nigh! Ah!

WAGNER. *(Coolly.)*

Observe him! 'Tis but a friar, 'tis not a spectre,
Muttering his prayers as he his rosary fingers.
Come hence, good master!

*(*FAUST *and* WAGNER *retire. The friar follows them.)*

SOPRANO CHORUS. *(From afar).*

The hansome young fellows
Have come to the dancing;
The dark ones, the fair ones,
Go whirling around!

TENOR CHORUS. *(Very distant.)*

Ah!

[*Almost out of hearing.*

(Scene changes.)

SCENA: *Officina di* FAUST. *Alcova. Notte.*

FAUST *entrando. Il Frate grigio lo segue e si nasconde entro l' alcova.*

SCENE: *Laboratory of* FAUST. *Alcove. Night.*

FAUST *enters. The grey Friar follows him and hides in the alcove.*

ARIA.—FAUST.

Dai campi, dai prati,
Che innonda la notte,
Che innonda la notte,
Dai queti sentier
Ritorno e di pace,
Di calma profonda
Son pieno e di sacro mister.
Le torve passioni del core
Si assonnano in placido obblio,
Mi ferve soltanto l'amore dell' umo!
L' amore di dio!
Ah! Dai campi, dai prati
Ritorno verso
L'Evangel mi sento attratto,
M'accingo a me di tar.

(Apre un Vangelo posto su d'un alto leggio. Mentre s'accinge a meditare e scosso dall' urlo dal Frate che esce dall' alcova.)

FAUST.

Ola! Chi urla? Il frate! Che vegg'io
Divider la mia cella io t'acconsento,
Frate, se tu non muggi—
E che? Mi guarda e non fa motto.
Che orribile fantasma
Trascinai dietro di me?
Furia demonio o spettro, sarai mio!
Sulla tua razza è onnipotente il segno di Saloman.

(All' ultime parole di FAUST *il Frate si trasforma e appare* MEFISTOFELE *in abito da cavaliere con un mantello nero sul braccio.)*

MEF.

Che baccano? Messer, mi comandate.

FAUST.

Questo era dunque il nocciuol del frate!
Un cavalier! Mi fa rider la facezia!
Come ti chiami?

MEF

La domanda è inezia puerile
Per tal che gli argomenti
Sdegna del Verbo e crede solo agli Enti.

ARI —FAUST.

From the green fields, from the meadows,
Where are falling night's shadows,
Where are falling night's shadows;
From the pathways now stilled,
Return I with sweet peace,
With calm deep and holy.
With myst'ries divine I am filled;
The passions that raged in my bosom,
All sleep in a quiet oblivion.
My only emotion is love and devotion
To God and to man!
Ah! From the green fields, from the meadows,
I now return! and toward the Evangelist attracted,
I'll yield me to mark and learn.

*(*FAUST *opens a volume placed on a lectern. His meditations are broken by the Friar's shriek as he issues from the alcove.)*

FAUST.

What ho! who's calling? The Friar! How is this?
To share my cell with you, freely I consent,
Good friar, but do not roar so.
How's this? He looks, but makes no movement.
What is this horrid phantom,
Standing in my presence here?
If fiend, foul demon or spectre, thou art mine!
O'er all thy race the sign of Solomon is potent and sure.

(At these last words of FAUST, *the Friar throws off his disguise, and* MEFISTOFELES *appears in the garb of a knight, with a black cloak on his arm.)*

MEF.

What an uproar! Good sir, I await your orders.

FAUST.

This must, then, be the kennel of the friar!
A cavalier! Well, the jest excites my laughter.
What is your name, sir?

MEF.

Sir, your question is foreign and childish,
For one who the ideal scorneth,
Believing only in the real!

FAUST.

In voi, messeri, il nome ha tal virtù
Che rivela l'Essenza. Dimmi or su,
Chi sei tu dunque?

MEF.

Una parte vivente di quella forza
Che perpetuamente pensa il Male é fa il Bene.

FAUST.

E che dir vuole
Codesto giocco di strane parole?

MEF.

Son lo Spirito che nega
Sempre tutto; l'astro il fior.
Il mio ghigno e la mia bega
Turban gli ozi al Crëator
Voglio il Nulla e del Creato
La ruina universal.
E atmosfera mia,
E atmosfera mia vital
Ciò che chiamasi peccato,
Morte e mal!
Rido e avvento questa sillaba: "No!"
Struggo, tento, ruggo sibilo—"No!"
Mordo, invischio, struggo, tento ruggo, sibilo.
Fischio! Fischio! Fischio! Fischio! Eh!

(Fischia violentemente colle dita fra le labbra.)

Parte son d'una latèbra
Del gran Tutto: Oscurità
Son figliuol della Tenèbra
Che Tenèbra tornorerà.
S'or la luce usurpa e afferra
Il mio scettro a ribellion,
Poco andrà e sua tenzon,
V'è sul Sol, v'è sul Sol,
V'è sul Sole la sulla Terra.
Distruzion!
Rido e avvento questa sillaba: "No!"
Struggo, tento, ruggo e sibilo—"No!"
Mordo invischio, fischio! fischio! fischio! etc. Eh!

(Fischia violentemente.)

DUO.—FAUST & MEFISTOFLE.

FAUST. (*Recit.*)

Strano figlio del Caos!

MEF.

E tu, se brami farti mio socio,
Di buon grado accetto fin da quest' ora
E tuo compar mi chiamo, o se ti piace,
Tuo schiavo, too servo.

FAUST.

Qualti patti in ricambio adempier dèggio?

MEF.

V' è tempo a sciò,

FAUST.

No; i patti e parla chiaro.

MEF.

Io qui mi lego a tuoi servigie
Senza tregua accorro alle tue voglie;
Ma laggiù (m'intendi?) la vece muterà.

FAUST.

Nay, but in you, sir, the true name may have pow'r
To reveal the true escence,
Tell me, then, at once who you are.

MEF.

I am only a portion of that great force
That always and forever thinketh ill but well doeth.

FAUST,

And what, then, meaneth
This subtile playing with words so peculiar?

MEFIS.

I'm the Spirit that denieth
All things, always—stars or flow'rs;
That by sneers and strife supplieth
Cause to vex the Heavenly powers.
I'm for Nought; and for creation,
Ruin, universal death!
And my life, my breath,
And my very life and breath,
Is what here they call transgression,
Sin and Death!
Shouting and laughing out this word I throw: "No!
Wasting, roaring, hissing, on I go—"No!"
Sland'ring, soiling, wasting, howling, hissing on I go,
Whist'ling, whist'ling, whist'ling, whist'ling! Eh!

(He whistles loudly, with his fingers between his lips.)

Part am I of that condition,
Of the whole obscurity,
Child of darkness and ambition,
Shadows, hiding, wait for me.
If the light usurps, contending,
On my rebel scepter's right,
Not prolonged will be the fight;
Over sun, over earth,
Over sun and earth is pending
Endless night!
Shouting and laughing out this word I throw: "No!
Blasting, soiling, roaring, on I go—"No!"
Wasting, spoiling, whist'ling, whist'ling, etc. Eh!

(He whistles violently as before.)

DUO.—FAUST & MEFISTOFELES.

FAUST.

Thou strange offspring of night!

MEF.

Shouldst thou desire to be my companion,
With great pleasure I assent from this moment;
And thy compeer thoul't call me, if it pleases thee,
Thy slave or thy servant.

FAUST.

And what's the bargain I must in turn agree to?

MEF.

There's time for that.

FAUST.

No; the bargain and speak distinctly.

MEF.

I here do bind me to thy good service,
Ready to obey thee, and meet thy wishes;
But below (you heed me?) our places will be chang'd

FAUST.

Per l' altra vita mon mi turba pensier
Se tu mi doni un' ora di riposo,
In cui s'acque ti l'alma.
Se sveli al mio bajo pensier
Me stesso e il mondo.
So avvien ch'io dica all' attimo fuggente:
Arrestati seibello! Allor ch'ie muoia
E m' inghiotta l'averno!

MEF.

Sta ben! (*Si danno la mano.*)

FAUST.

Venga il contratto!

MEF.

Top è già fatto!
Fin da sta notte nel l'orgie ghiotte
Del mio messer da camerier,
De camerierre lo serviorò.
Da camerier, da camerier, ecc., ecc.

FAUST.

Fin da sta notte nell' orgie ghiotte,
Nell' orgie ghiotte del suo messer, ecc.
(*Recit.*) E quando s' incomincia?

MEF.

Tosto!

FAUST.

Or ben, presto a noi dove andiam?

MEF.

Dove t' aggrada.

FAUST.

Come s' esce di qua?
Dove i cavalli, le carrozze. i staffier?

MEF.

Pur ch' io distenda questo mantel,
Noi viaggeremo sull' aria.

FINE DEL ATTO PRIMO.

FAUST.

About the future, not a thought do I give.
If thou dost bring me one hour
Of peace and quiet, in which may rest my spirit;
If thou wilt myself and the world unveil before me;
If I should haply say to the moment flying:
"Stay thee, for thou art blissful!
Ah! let me die then,
And let hell there engulf me!

MEF. (*Gives his hand.*)

'Tis well!

FAUST.

Now for the contract!

MEF.

Done 'tis already!
Then from to-night forth, in all the revels,
Master thou'lt be, as you'll see, and servant I'll be,
Serving my master right faithfully!
Servant I'll be, etc.

FAUST.

Then from to-night forth,
In all the revels, master I'll be, etc.
(*Recit.*) And when shall we commence this?

MEF.

Now!

FAUST.

'Tis well; be it now; and where to?

MEF.

Where it may suit you.

FAUST.

By what means shall we go?
Where are the horses, the postillions, the coach?

MEF.

I've but to stretch my cloak; in this wise
Up thro' the air we shall journey.

END OF THE FIRST ACT.

ATTO SECONDO. ACT SECOND.

IL GARDINO. (THE GARDEN.)

SCENE.—*A garden of rustic appearance.* FAUST *(under the name of* HENRY*).* MARGARET, MEFISTOFELES, MARTHA. *They stroll here and there in couples.*

MARG.

Cavaliero illustre e saggio,
Come mai vi può allettar
La fanciulla del villaggio
Col suo rustico parlar?

FAUST.

Dalle labbra im'porporate
Spandi accento sovruman.
Parla, parla. (*Baciandole la mano.*)

MARG.

Ah! non baciate
Questa ruvida mia man!
(*Con risoluto.*) No! No! cavalier! [*Passano.*

MEF (*a* MARTA.)

Sta ben al nubilĕ, correr giocondo,
In traccia d' ilari venture, il mondo.

MARTA.

Ah, ah! Ah, ah!

MEF.

Ma quando lugubre tempo verrà
Vecchio nel vedovo letto morrà.
Pur troppo! e trepido
Vedo quell' ora!

MARTA.

Baie! pensateci.
C'è tempo ancora.
C'è tempo ancor, c'è tempo ancor!

FAUST.

Mi perdona l'ardimento
Che dal labbro mi sfuggi
Quando il magioco portento
Del tuo viso m' apparì.

MARG.

Fu! dolente, fui turbata,
Dubitai nel mio pensier
Che fanciulla scostumata
Mi credeste cavalier,
Piansi molto, piansi molto,
Ma rimasemi nel cor
Sempre fiso il vostro volto.
Segui, segui, o mio tesor!

MEF.

Da un antichissimo detto s'impara
Che moglie saggia e cosa rara.
Rara davver!

MARG. (*With simplicity.*)

Cavalier, with wisdom laden,
What attractions can you see
In a simple village maiden
With her rustic speech, like me?

FAUST. (*Tenderly and fervidly.*)

From those crimson lips unfolding,
Flows an accent past all art.
Speak! Ah, speak now! [*Kisses her hand.*

MARG.

Ah! do not kiss this hand so rough,
(*With resolution.*) Or we must part. No, no, cavalier!
[*They retire.*

MEF. (*To* MARTHA.)

Well may the young and fair run without censure,
Thro'out the world in search of gay adventure.

MARTHA. (*Laughing.*) Ah, ah! Ah, ah!

MEF.

But when the sorrowful time shall draw nigh,
I on my widowed bed shall lonely die.
Too soon, alas! I see that hour approaching.

MARTHA.

Bah, good sir, think not so,
Time enough, surely,
There's time enough, ere you will go.
(*FAUST & MARGARET return. MEF. & MARTHA retire.*,

FAUST.

Pray, now, pardon me the boldness
That my daring lips have shown;
When the magic of thy charming face
Before me first was thrown.

MARG.

I was troubled, disconcerted—
In my mind some doubts appeared,
That for some maid, fooled, deserted,
You mistook me, sir, I feared.
Much I wept, my hope had fainted;
But still on my heart remain
Your dear features, strongly painted.

FAUST.

Speak, beloved! Say it again!
(*MARGARET and FAUST pass out.*)

MEF.

From an old proverb book, comes this odd saying—
"That wives with wise heads are rarely straying."
Rarely—'tis true!

MARTA.

Davver? nè in trappola cadeste ancor?

MEF.

Non so credetelo, che sia l'amor.

MARTA.

Né mai d' un palpito, Nè mai d'un sogno
V' arse bisogno fascinator?

MEF.

Non so, credetelo, che sia l'amor. [*Passano.*

MARG.

Dimmi se credi, Enrico, nella religione.

FAUST.

Non vo' turbar le fedi delle coscienze buone
D' altro parliam;
Darei perchè amo, fanciulla, sangue e vita.

MARG.

Non basta—creder bisogna,
E a nulla tu credi, Enrico.

FAUST.

Ascolta verzoso angelo mio!
Chi oserebbe affermare tal detto: credo in Dio?
La parole dei santi son beffe al ver ch'io chiedo,
E qual uomo oserebbe tanto da dir: non credo?

MARTHA.

'Tis true? Have you never fallen as yet in the sweet snare?

MEF.

What love may be, I nothing know or care.

MARTHA.

Have you never felt the bliss, the tender yearning,
The passion burning of love's sweet snare?

MEF.

What love may chance to be, I neither know nor care
[*They retire.*

(MAR. *returning with* FAUST.)

MAR. (*With great simplicity.*)

Now, tell me, dearest, have you faith in true religion?

FAUST.

I would not vex the conscience of one so good and trustful.
Change we theme— [love you.
My life I would give you, dear maid, because I

MAR. (*Reprovingly.*)

Nay, tell me, faith you have need of,
And you, love, believe in nothing!

FAUST. (*Tenderly.*)

Now, hear me, my angel—I'll not deceive! [lieve'
Who would dare to affirm in his conscience, I be-
All the words of the pious are jests that I receive not,
Yet what man in his senses dares to declare, "I believe not"?

Andante sostenuto.

Colma il tuo cor d'un palpito
Ineffabile e vero d'amor.
E chiama poi quell' estasi,
Natura! Amor! Mistero!
Vita! Dio!
Non è che fumo e fola,
In paragon del senso
Il nome e la parola. Ah! chia ma tu, ecc.

MARG.

Con vien che veda addio.

FAUST.

Dimmi, in casa sei sola sovente?

MAR. (*Semplicemente.*)

E piccioletta la nostra famigliola.
Io veglio all' orto, al desco ed allo staio,
Attedo ad ogni cura filò sull' arcolaio.
E assai minuziosa la mamma, eppur beate
Placidamente passo tutte le mie giornate.

FAUST.

Di' non potrò giammai dolce un'ora d'amore,
Viver teco e confondere il mio cuor col tuo cuore?

Flood thou thy heart with all the bliss
That from true and ardent love doth proceed,
And call that rapt'rous ecstacy,
As Nature! Love! and Mystery!
Life and heaven!
Both are but empty notions!
Tested by sense and wisdom
They are but words—emotions! Ah! name, etc.

MAR.

Farewell, I now must be going.

FAUST.

Tell me—alone in your home are you often?

MAR. (*With simplicity.*)

But small affairs are our quiet home and household.
I keep the garden, thus every day beginning;
Attend my round of duties (*smiling*), then sit me down to spinning.
My mother's over-careful it may be, yet happy ever,
I pass my days serenely, harrassed by trouble never.

FAUST.

Say, may I not look forward to one hour of pleasure,
When our hearts may in union beat to love's blissful measure?

MAR.

Non dormo sola é in .ieve sopor mia madre giace:
S'ella t' udisse, credo ne morrei.

FAUST.

Datti pace. A te.
(Porgendole un' ampollina.)
Di questo succo tre sole goccie ponno
Addormentare in placido, in letargico sonno.

MAR.

Porgi—nè può venirne, alcun male a mia madre?

FAUST.

Nessuno, nessuno!
Angiol soave dalle guancie leggiadre.

MAR.

Dio clemente, nuova, ignara
Son del mondo dell' amore;
Sento un' aura arcana e cara
Che mi penetra nel corre.
Ah! sento, ah! sento un' aura arcana e cara.

MARTHA.

Ah, Davver? nè in trappola,
Nè in trappola cadeste ancor. Ah! ecc.

FAUST.

E l'anelito superno,
Il miracolo divino della vita!
Senza freno, senza freno,
Senza fine! è il miracolo d'amor Si!

MEF.

Non so, credetelo,
Che sia l'amore non so, credetelo
Non so, credetolo, sia l'more.
Moglie saggia è cosa rara davver, davver!

FAUST.

Ah! sento un' aura arcana e cara.

MARG.

Addio! Fuggo, fuggo, lesta, lesta, ecc.
Ah, ah, ah, ecc. T'amo, t'amo!

FAUST.

Resta, resta, Margherita! ecc.
T'amo, t'amo!

MARTA.

Corri, corri, lesto, lesto,
T'amo, t'amo

MEF.

Marta, Marta, Marta, Marta! ecc.
Tu sei côlta, tu sei côlta.
Ah, ah, ah, ecc. T'amo!

LA NOTTE DEL SABBA.

SCENA.—*Scena deserta e selvaggia nella vallea di Schirk, costeggiata dagli spaventosi culmini del Brocken (monte delle streghe). I sinistri profili delle roccie staccano in nero sul cielo grigio, un' aurora rossiccia di luna illumina stranamente la scena. Una caverna da un lato. Il picco di Rosstrappe a sinistra. Il vento soffia nei burroni; poi la voce di* MEFISTOFELE *che aizzia* FAUST *a salir la montagna.*

MEF. *(Assai lontano con suono lungo e sotterraneo.)*
Su cammina, cammina, cammina;
Negro è il cielo, scoscesa è la china;
Su cammina, cammina, cammina!

MAR.

Alone I may not receive thee, my mother sleeps but lightly;
If she should hear thee, I should die, believe me!

FAUST. *(Offering a phial.)*
Do not worry—take this;
And of its contents, if but three drops are taken,
They will a slumber produce from which it will be hard to awaken. [MARTHA & MEFIS *return.*

MAR. *(Takes phial.)*
Give it—no harm will come. you are sure, to my mother?

FAUST.

No, surely; believe me— [Ah, ah!
Naught but a quiet sleep, my angel; none other.

MAR.

Pitying heaven! nothing knowing
Of the world's ways, or of loving;
Airs mysterious feel I blowing,
Whence my heart new bliss is proving.
Ah! o'er me I feel mysterious, etc.

MARTHA. *(As if murmuring.)*
Ah! is't true that you have ne'er
As yet fallen in love's snare? Ah, yes!

FAUST.

'Tis the height of bliss terrestrial,
'Tis the mystery celestial of our being.
Curbless, restless, upward tending,
Never ending—'tis the mystery of love. Yes!

MEF.

What is love I know not;
Naught I know what love may be, nor do I care
Wives with wise heads are a sight truly rare, etc.

FAUST.

I feel mysterious airs o'er me blowing.

MAR. *(Freeing herself from* FAUST.)
Farewell! homeward hieing, swiftly flying, etc.
(Breaking into laughter.)
Ah, ah, ah, etc. I love thee, love thee!

FAUST *(Following* MAR.)
Stay thee, stay thee, Margaret darling! etc.
I love thee, love thee!

MARTHA.

Hurry, skurry, sprightly, lightly, etc.
(Laughing.) Ah, ah, etc. I love thee, love thee

MEF. *(Follows* MARTHA.)
Martha, Martha, Martha, Martha! ecc.
(Catching MARTHA.) I have caught you, etc.
I love thee!

THE NIGHT OF THE SABBATH.

SCENE.—*A lonely, wild spot in the valley of Schirk, among the higher summits of the Brocken. Black rocks against a grey sky. Red moonrise. At one side, a cavern; to the left, the Rosstrappe. Wind whistling through the openings.* MEFISTOFELES *helping* FAUST *to climb the mountain.*

MEF. *(With tones hollow and subterranean.)*
Come up higher, and higher, and higher;
To the summit we're fast getting nigher;
Come up higher, and higher, and higher!

MEF.

Su cammina, cammina, cammina,
Che lontano, lontano, lontan
S'erge il mon te del vecchio Satan.
Bujo è il cielo, scoscesa è la china;
Su cammina, cammina, ecc.

CORO.

Cammina, cammina, cammina, ecc.

(Appariscono dei fuochi fatui, uno di questi si dirige alla volta di FAUST e MEFISTOFELE.)

FAUST. Folletto!
MEF. Folletto!

FAUST.

Folletto, folletto, folletto!
Velloce leggier,
Che splendi soletto
Per l'ermo sentier,
A noi t' avvicina,
Che buia è la china.
Che buia è la china, ecc.
Folletto! Folletto!
A noi t'avvicena!

MEF.

Cammina! Cammina!

CORO. Cammina, cammina, cammina, ecc.

(MEFISTOFELE e FAUST appariranno sovra un' alta roccia isolati ed immobili.)

MEF.

Ascolta! S'agita il bosco e gli alti pini antichi,
Cozzan furenti colle giganti braccia.

CORO. Ah! Ah!

MEF.

Ascolto! Ascolto!
Ad imo della valle un ululato
Di mille vocci odo sonar.

CORO. Ah! Ah!

MEF.

S'accosts l'infernale congrega—
Oh! meraviaglia!

CORO. Ah! Ah!

MEF.

Già i nembi, il monte,
Le boscaglie, i cielime!

CORO. (STREGONI.)

Rampiamo, ramapiamò che il tempo ci gabba,
E il ballo perdiamo di Re Belzebù
E notte fatale la notte del Sabba;
Il primo che sale ha un premio di più,
E notte tremenda la notte del Sabba;
Il primo che ascenda ha un primo di più.

TUTTI.

Su! Su! Su! Su! ecc.

CORO. (STREGONI.)

E notte tremenda la notte del Sabba.
Su svelti, su forti che il tempo ci gabba,
Le nostra consorti son giunte lassu.
E notte tremenda la notte del Sabba,
E il primo che ascenda ha un premio di più, ecc.
Su! Su! Su! Su! ecc.

(Irrompendo tutti frenetiocamente sulla scena.)

MEF.

Come up higher, and higher, and higher,
Farther yet, 'tis more dreary the road
That will lead us to Satan's abode.
Dark the sky is, the ascent grows steeper,
Come up higher and higher, and higher.

CHORUS.

Up higher, and higher, and higher, etc.

(Lambent flames appear; one flies in front of FAUST, the other in front of MEF.)

FAUST. Ah, wild fire!
MEF. Ah, wild fire!

FAUST.

Ah, wild fire, wild fire, pallid light!
Now so dim, now so bright;
Flash o'er us thy ray, to illumine our way—
Come nigher, come nigher,
For dark is the ascent, as higher, and higher
We're upward advancing,
Come, flame, wildly dancing,
Come nigher and nigher!

MEF.

Come up higher and higher! *(With a roar.)*

CHORUS. Up higher, and higher, higher, etc.

(They come out on an eminence, motionless and solitary.)

MEF.

Now hearken! Hear how the pines of the forest, tall and ancient,
Hurtle and clash their giant arms together!

CHORUS. Ah! Ah!

MEF.

Now, hark you, and listen! *(Excitedly.)*
Below there, in the valley,
I hear a thousand shrill voices, shouting loudly, resound.

CHORUS. Ah!

MEF.

The infernal crowd approaches still nearer:
Oh, what a wonder!

CHORUS. Ah!

MEF. *(with infernal joy.)*

The clouds and mountains,
Forest trees and fountains,
All are thundering around wonderful anthems.

WITCHES' CHORUS.

Come onward, come onward, for time may deceive us
King Belzebub's dance we shall lose, 'twill be o'er,
The night of our Sabbath to miss would be gri'vious,
The first who arrives will have one prize the more.
The night of our Sabbath to miss, etc.

WITCHES & WIZARDS.

On! On! On! On!

WIZARDS' CHORUS.

A wild, stirring scene is the night of our Sabbath,
Up nimbly, up quickly, for time may deceive us,
Already our comrades have reached the wild plain.
The feast of our Sabbath's an orgie tremendous.
The first who arrives there, etc.
On! On! On! etc.

(They burst frantically upon the scene.)

CORO.

Siam salve in tutta l'eternità!
Sì! Saboè, Saboè, Saboè! ecc.

MEF. (*Fendendo la folla.*)

Largo, largo, a Mefistofele, al vostro Re!
O razza putrida vuota di fè.
Che ognun m'adori ed umile
Si prostri al Re. O razza, ecc.

CORO. (*Inginocchiati in circolo attorno a* MEF.)

Ci prostriamo a Mefistofele, al nostro Re:
Ognuno atterrasi dinanzi a te.

MEF. (*Su d'un sasso in forma di trono.*)

Popoli! e scettro e clamide mon date al Re sovrano.
La formidabil mano vuota dovrò serrar?

CORO.

(*Porgendo una clamide a* MEF.)

Ecco la clamide, non t'adirar,
Or t'ubbidiscono ciel, terra e mar.
Non t'adirar.

MEF.

Ho soglio, ho scettro e despota
Son del mio regno fiero.
Ma voglio il mondo intero nel pugno mio serrar.

CORO.

(*Correndo intorno ad una caldaia che sta nel fondo della scena. Breve danza.*)

Sotto la pentola corri a soffiar,
Entro la pentola corri a mischiar!
Entro la pentola corri a danzar, ecc.

(*Porgendo à* MEF. *un globo di vetro.*)

Eccoti, o principe il mondo inter!

MEF.

(*Col globo di vetro in mano.*)

Ecco il mondo,
Vuoto e tondo, s'alza,
Scende, balza, e splende.
Fa coro le intorno al sole.
Trema, rugge, dà e di strugge
Ora sterile or fecondo.
Ecco il mondo!
Sul so grosso, anticodosso
V'è una schiatta e sozza e matta,
Fiera, vile, ria, sottile,
Che ad ogn' ora si divora.
Dalla cima sino al fondo—
Del reo mondo!
Fola vana è a lei Satana,
Riso e scherno è a lei l'inferno.
Scherno e riso il paradiso.
Oh, per Dio! che or rido anch' io
Nel pensar ciò che le ascondo—
Ah, ah, ah, ecc! Ecco il mondo!

(*Getta con impeto il globo di vetro che si frange.*)

CORO.

Riddiamo! Reddiamo!
Riddiamo, Riddiamo! che il mondo è ca duto!
Riddiamo, Riddiamo! che il mondo è per duto!
Sul morti frantumi del globe fatal.
S accenda, s'intrecci la ridda infernal, ecc.

CHORUS.

We're saved through endless eternity!
Yes! Saboè! Saboè! Saboè! etc.

MEF. (*Cleaving the throng.*)

Room, make room for Mefistofles, bow to your king!
Race of corruption, homage here bring!
Down before me, kneel, adore me,
Your ruler and king.

CHORUS. (*Kneel in a circle around* MEF.)

Here we bow to Mefistofeles, to our great king,
Our homage humbly before thee we bring!

MEF.

(*Seated upon a rock shaped like a throne.*)

Subjects all! the staff and robes of state
Do you not give your sov'reign?
Here, in my grasp despotic, must I have naught to hold?

CHORUS.

(*Presenting a cloak to* MEFISTOFELES.)

Here is the robe of state; anger forbear;
All things are thrall to thee, earth, sea and air.
Anger forbear.

MEF.

I've sceptre, and throne, and robe of state,
With pride I hold my kingdom;
But all the wide creation my grasp would fain enfold.

CHORUS.

(*Circling about a cauldron in the back of the scene.*)

Under the cauldron we kindle the fire,
In the black cauldron we mix up the mire,
Over the cauldron we dance and conspire, etc.

(*Presenting a glass globe to* MEF.)

Lo! here, O great monarch, this world entire!

MEF.

(*With a globe of glass in his hand.*)

Lo! the world here stands,
A bright sphere rising,
Setting, whirling, glancing,
Round the sun in circles dancing;
Trembling, toiling, yielding, spoiling,
Want and plenty by turns enfold it—
This world, behold it!
On its surface, by time abraded,
Dwelleth a vile race, defiled, degraded—
Abject, haughty, cunning, naughty,
Carrying war and desolation
From the top to the foundation
Of creation.
For them Satan has no being,
They scorn, with laughter, a hell hereafter.
And heavenly glory as idle story.
Powers eternal! I'll join their laugh infernal;
Thinking o'er their deeds diurnal.
Ah, ah! Ah, ah! etc. Lo! the world here

(*Throws down the globe and dashes it to pieces.*)

CHORUS.

Now turn we, now turn we!
In circles we're turning, the world now is shattered,
We're turning, and turning, its atoms are scattered;
And over its fragments to ashes that burn,
In circles infernal we'll gleefully turn, etc.

FAUST.

Stupor! Stupor!
Là nel lontano, nel nebuloso ciel
Una fanciulla pallida mesta, la scerni?
Il piede lento conduce e di catene avviato!
Ah! pietosa vision ma rassomiglia
Quella dolce figura a Margherita

MEF.

Torci il guardo, torci il guardo!
Quello è spettro seduttor.
È fantasma maliardo,
Che a chi il fissa ammorba il cor.
Torci il guardo, anima illusa,
Dalla testa di Medusa!

FAUST.

Quell' occhio da celeste,
Spalancato cadavericamente!
E il bianco sen che tanti ebbe da me baci d'amore!
Si e Margherita, si, l'angelo mio!

MEF.

Torci il guardo, nella fata,
Sogna ognun colei che amò.

FAUST.

Ah! strano vezzo il collo le circonda
D'una riga sanguigna?

MEF.

Ha la testa distaccata,
Perseo fu che la tagliò.

CORO. (*Ridda e fuga infernale.*)

Ah! Su! riddiamo, riddiamo, che il tempo ci gabba,
Sui vecchi rottami del globo fatal;
E notte tremenda la notte del Sabba,
Rimbombi sul monte la ridda infernal.
Sabba, Sabba, Saboè! ecc.
Riddiam, riddiamo, riddiamo, riddiamo ecc.
Saboè har Sabbah! Riddiam, riddiamo.
Sui vecchi rottami del globo fatal.
Si! Ridiamo, che il tempo ci gabba,
Rimbombi sul monte la ridda infernal, ecc.

FINE DEL ATTO SECONDO.

FAUST.

Benumbed! Amazed!
There, in the distance, against the murky sky,
Seest thou a maiden, pallid and sorrowful seeming?
Her foot but slowly doth move, for with a chain 'tis fettered?
Ah! a pitiful sight! [poor dead Margaret.
Those lovely features seem to me to resemble my

MEF.

Turn away, then, turn your glances,
'Tis an empty dream, and vain,
'Tis a phantom of your fancies,
Nurtured in a fevered brain;
Turn; your glances false is its showing,
From Medusa's head growing.

FAUST.

Those eyes of heavenly azure
Are now sunken and like a corpses;
Shrunken, too, the breast
That often from my lips love's kisses knew!
(*With great passion.*) Yes; 'tis my dead Margaret,
My angel dear—ah! my angel dear!

MEF.

Turn your glances! Thus 'tis fated,
Dreams evey one that love doth know.

FAUST.

Ah! what is that that round her throat
A line doth draw, as if bleeding?

MEF.

Seemingly decapitated—
Perseus 'twas that struck the blow.

CHORUS. (*Infernal dance and flight.*)

Ah! Round again we're turning
The time doth befriend us;
We dance on the ruin and rack of the world;
The night of our Sabbath,
Our doings stupendous, [hurled.
From mountain to mountain their echoes are
Sabba, Sabba, Saboè etc.
In circles turning, and turning, and turning—
Saboé har Sabbah! Round and round,
Over the ruin and rack of the fated old world, etc.
Yes! Turning and turning the night doth befriend us, [sound.
With echoes tremendous the mountains re-

END OF ACT SECOND.

ATTO TERZO. ACT THIRD.

MORTE DI MARGHERITA. (DEATH OF MARGARET.)

(MEFISTOFLES. She is condemned!—GOETHE. A prison.)

SCENE.—*A Prison.* MARGARET *extended upon a heap of straw, singing, with senses wandering. Night. A lighted lamp hangs against the wall. A grating in the back of the cell.*

MAR.

L'altra notte in fondo al mare
Il mio bimbo hanno gitttao,
Or per farmi delirare
Dicon ch'io l' abbia affogato.
L'aura e fredda, il carcer fosco,
E la mesta anima mia
Come il passero del bosco
Vola via. Ah, pietà di me!
In funereo sopore
E mia madre addormentata,
E per colmo dell' orrore
Dicon ch' io l' abbia attoscata.
L'aura é fredda, il carcer fosco,
E la mesta anima mia
Come il passero del bosco
Vola via. Ah! pietà di me!

FAUST. (*Outside the grating.*)

Salvala!

MEF. (*Fuori del cancello.*)

E chi la spinse nell' abisso?
Io? o tu? Ciò che posso farò.
Ecco le chiavi. Dormono i carcerieri,
I puledri fatati son pronti per la fuga.

(*MEF. Porge un mazzo di chiavi ed esce.*)

(*FAUST entra in carcere.*)

MAR.

Dio di pietà! son essi eccoli, aita!
Durra cosa è il morir.

FAUST.—(*Recit.*)

Pace! Pace! Io son un cheti salva.

MAR. (*Affannosa.*)

Un uom—tu sei. Di carità, l'abbi per me.

ARIA.—MAR.

(*Wandering mentally, and singing.*)

To the sea, O night of sadness!
They my babe took and in it threw him!
Now, to drive me on to madness,
They declare 'twas I who slew him!
Cold the air is, the dark cell narrow,
And my spirit, broken to-day,
Like the timid woodland sparrow,
Longs to fly far, far away. Father, pity me!
In a deathly slumber falling,
Died my mother—no aid could save her;
And, to crown the woe appalling,
They declare I poison gave her.
Cold the air is, the cell dark and narrow,
And my sad heart, broken to-day, etc.

FAUST. (*Outside the grating.*)

Save her life!

MEF. (*Hoarsely. Outside the grating.*)

To this condition who has brought her?
I or you? I will do what I can.
Here is the cell key,—sleeping are all the jailors,
And the coursers infernal for speedy flight is ready.

(*MEF. opens the cell and retires.*)

(*FAUST enters prison.*)

MAR.

Merciful heaven! behold them coming to save me!
Oh, 'tis hard thus to die!

FAUST. (*Recit—long pause.*)

Hush thee! calm thee! I have come to save thee!

MAR, (*Pettishly.*)

A man thou art—have charity, and pity me.

FAUST.

Silenzio! Margherita!

MAR.

Cielo! Ah, parla ancora! Ah, parla!
Ah, tu mi salvi! Ah, m'hai salvata!
Ecco la strada è questa
Dov'io ti vidi per la prima volta.
Ecco il giardin di Marta!

FAUST.

Ah, vieni! Ah, vieni!

MAR.

Resta ancor! Resta ancor!

FAUST.

T'affretta o a prezzo tremendo pagherem l'indugio.

MAR.

E non mi baci—e non mi baci!
Ah, le tue labbra son gelo—
Che festi dell'amor tuo?

FAUST.

Cessa!

MAR.

Tu mi togli pietoso alle catene?
E ignori chi tu salvi, o pietoso?
Ho avvelenata la mia povera madre,
Ed ho affogato il fantolino mio
Qua la tua mano.
Vien vo'narrar ti il te tro ordin di tombe.
Che doman scaverai.
Là fra le zolle più verdeggianti.
Stenderai mia madre
Nel più bel sitodel cimiter—
Discosto ma pur vicino—
Scaverai la mia, la povera fossa
E il mio bambino poserà sul mio sen.

FAUST.

Deh! ti scongiuro, fuggiamo.

MAR.

No. Sta l'inferno a quella porta;
Ah! perchè fuggi? perchè non t'arresti?
Non ti posso seguir.
E poi, la vita per me è dolor;
Che far sulla terra?
Mendicare il mio pane a frusto a frusto
Dovrò colla coscienza päurosa de' miei de litti.

FAUST.

Be silent! Dearest Margaret! (*With effusion.*)

MAR.

Mercy! Once more repeat—ah, say it!
Ah, thou wilt save me Saved already!
(*Wanderingly.*) See you that this the street is
Where for the first time I beheld your features?
There, too, is Martha's garden.

FAUST. (*Anxiously.*)

Ah, hasten, dearest!

MAR. (*Tranquilly.*)

Stay, yet; one moment, stay.

FAUST.

Ah! haste thee, or this delay haply may cost us dearly.

MAR. (*With affectionate apprehension.*)

Thou dost not kiss me—thou dost not kiss me?
Ah, cold and icy your lips are. (*Tragically.*)
What have you done with your true love?

FAUST. Cease this!

MAR.

You would take me, in pity, from my prison?
You know not whom your pity is saving.
My own poor mother they declare I did poison,
And half suffocated my darling little babe—
[*Grieviously.*
Here—give your hand, love.
Come, I will tell you the gloomy order of burial,
That to-morrow shall witness;
There, where the grass is freshest and greenest,
You will lay my mother—
Of all the churchyard the fairest place;
And near it—not too far distant—
Hollow out for me, too, my last resting-place lonely,
And my dear baby on my bosom you'll lay.

FAUST.

Ah! I beseech you, let's fly now!

MAR.

No! Hell is just beyond that portal.
Ah! Why then fly we? Why not stay beside me?
I can never follow thee.
Moreover, existence is pain for me.
What, then, should I live for?
Forced to beg for my living from door to door,
With my guilty conscience bringing before me my dark offences.

DUO.—FAUST e MARGHERITA.

FAUST.

Rivolgi a me lo sguardo!
Ah Odi la voce dell'amor che prega!
Vieni fuggiam.

MAR.

Sì fuggiamo!
Già sognoun incantato asil di pace,
Dove soavemente uniti ognor vivrem.

FAUST e MAR.

Lontano, lontano, lontano
Sui flutti d'un ampio, oceàno
Fra i roridi effluvi del mar,
Fra l'alghe, fra i fior, fru le palme,
Il porto dell' intime calme,
L'azzurra isoletta m'appar.
M'appare sul cielo sereno
Ricinta d'un arcobaleno
Specchiante il sorriso del sol.
La fuga dei liberi amanti
Speranti, migranti, raggianti
Dirige a quel l'isola il volo,
A quell' isola il vol.
Lontano, lontano, lontano, lontano.

MEF.

Sorge il dì!

MAR.

Ah! Satana rugge!

FAUST. (*Disperatamente.*)

Ah! deh! t'affretta il tempo fugge!

MARG. (*a* FAUST.)

Ah! no, non lasciarmi in abbandono!

MEF.

Squilla già da quelle porte
La fanfara, la fanfara della morte.

MAR. (*Staccandos da* FAUST.)

Ahi me! gran Dio tu allontana la mia tentazion!
Mi strazian le membra condure ritorte.
O Dio, tu m'aiuta! mi guidano amorte.
Ah! Già sui mio capo la scure sul mio brillò!

FAUST.

Serena fanciulla lo spirto sconvolto,
Ch'io vegga tranquillo quel pallido volto,
Pon freno alla foga de' vani sospiri.
C'è d'uopo fuggir. Ah sì! c'è d'uopo fuggir!
Ah! non fossi mai nato!

MEF. (*Accanto a* FAUST.)

Cessate, cessate le vane parole,
Dal ciel d'orïente già levasi il sole,
De' neri puledri già s'ode il nitrire,
C'è d'upo fuggir, fuggiam!

MAR.

Chi s'erge? chi s'erge della terra?
E il mostro! Misericordia! in questo santo asilo.
Che vuole il maledetto?
Ah! lo discaccia, è forse me ch'ei vuol!

FAUST.

Ah! vieni, e vivi, deh! vivi Margherita.

MEF.

Mi segui, o entrambi v'abbandono alla mannaia.

DUO.—FAUST & MARGARET.

FAUST.

Upon me turn thy glances!
Ah! hear the voice of love beseeching
Come, now, let's fly.

MAR.

Yes; we will fly now.
I've dreamed of an abode of peace enchanting
Where we may happily united ever live.

FAUST & MARGARET.

Away from strife and commotion,
O'er waves of a wide-spreading ocean,
'Mid perfumes exhaled by the sea,
'Mid palm-trees and flowers in profusion,
The portal of peace and seclusion,
The blue isle seems waiting for me.
There skies in their beauty transcendent
Seem girt with a rainbow resplendent,
Reflecting the sun's loving smile.
The flight of all hearts that are loving,
And hopeful, and moving, and roving
Is turned toward that life-giving island,
That life-giving isle.
Away to that island far distant!

MEF. (*Appearing in the background.*)

Day has risen!

MAR.

Ah, 'tis Satan roaring!

FAUST. (*Desperately.*)

Ah, haste, I pray thee; the time is flying!

MAR. (*To* FAUST.)

Ah, no; do not leave me in my sorrow!

MEF.

From that portal dark appalling,
Sounds the trumpet note of death, now for thee calling [away.

MAR. (*Backing from* FAUST.)

Alas! O Heaven, from me turn this temptation
My limbs are distorted by instruments deadly.
O God, now sustain me! To death now they lead me.
Ah! the axe, already, yes, already doth fall on my head.

FAUST.

Oh, calm, now, my dearest, thy mind so excited.
That I may behold thy sad features hope-lighted,
Aside lay thy passion, thy sighing and weeping,
We quickly must fly Ah, yes!
Would I had ne'er been born!

MEF. (*Approaches* FAUST.)

Now cease ye, now cease all these words unavailing,
The glow in the sky 'fore the sun now is paling;
The black steeds impatient are stamping and neighing. We quickly must fly—must fly!

MAR.

Who riseth? Who from the earth now riseth?
'Tis Satan! Oh show some mercy in this asylum holy.
What seeks the fiend accursed?
Ah! drive him forth, perchance for me he waits!

FAUST.

Ah! come and live still, yes, live still dearest Margaret.

MEF.

Come, follow me, or to the headsmen I will leave you.

(Light of dawn. MEFISTOFELES *goes to examine the grating.* MARGARET *lies exhausted and fainting in the arms of* FAUST.)

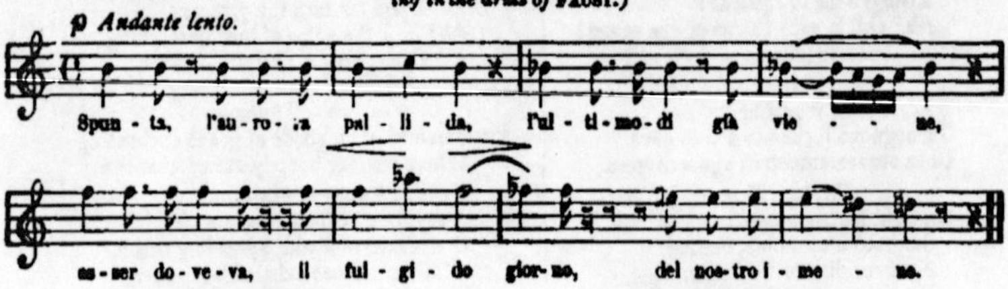

MAR.
Spunta l'aurora pallida,
L' ultimo di già viene,
Esser doveva il fulgido
Giorno del nostro imene.
Tutto è finito in vita!

FAUST.
O strazio crudel!

MAR.
Taci ad ognun s'asconda
S'asconda che amasti Margherita
E ch'io tie diedi il cor.
Ah! a questa moribonda perdonerai,
Signor, perdonerai Signor!
Padre Santo! mi salva e
Voi celesti proteggete questa che a voi si volge!

MEF.
E giudicata!

FAUST.
O strazio!

MAR.
Enrico, mi fai ribrezzo! *(Falls.)*

CORO. *(Dall alto.)*
E salve! E salve!

MEF.
A me, Faust!

(FAUST. e MEF. *scompaiono. Nel fondo il carnefice circondato da sgherri. Cala il sipario.)*

FINE DELLA PRIMA PARTE.

MAR.
Morning is lightly breaking,
Life's latest day is waking—
Thus should have been soon our bridal day
Morning, with splendor dawning,
But all with life now is ending.

FAUST.
O outrage cruel!

MAR.
Hush thee! from all eyes soon banished
Will be the Marg'ret who once adored thee,
Who to thy care gave her heart.
Ah! pardon me! Dying, I pray thee for pardon,
O Lord! Thy pardon grant, O Lord!
Holy Father! O save thou me!
Holy angels, kindly welcome one to your arms returning!

MEF.
They have condemned her!

FAUST.
O horror!

MAR. *(Falls.)*
Oh, Henry, thy sin is hateful!

CHORUS. *(Within.)*
She's saved! She's saved!

MEF.
Now come, Faust.

(FAUST *and* MEFISTOFELES *escape. In the background, the executioner appears with his escort.*

END OF PART FIRST.

ATTO QUARTO. ACT FOURTH.

THE NIGHT OF THE CLASSICAL SABBATH.

HELEN.—Tell me what I must do to learn that tender idiom. (GOETHE.—*Faust, Part Second.)*

SCENE.—*Shores of the Peneus, in the Vale of Tempe. Limpid water, with thickets of laurels and oleanders. The moon, at the zenith, sheds an enchanting light o'er the scene. A Doric temple at the left. In the background* HELEN *and* PANTALIS. *Groups of syrens.* FAUST *lies dozing on the flowery bank.*

ELENA.
La luna immobile innonda l'etere

PANTALIS. Canta.

ELENA.
D'un raggio pallido.

PAN.
Calido balsamo stillan le ramora dai

ELENA. Canta.

PAN
Cespi roridi.

ELENA.
Doridi e silfidi
Cigni e nereidi

PAN. Canta.

ELENA.
Vagan sull'alighe.
L'aura è serena,

PAN. Canta.

ELENA.
La luna è piena,
Canta, o sirena, la serenata!

PAN.
Canta, canta, o sirena; canta!

FAUST (*Dozing.*)
Elèna! Elèna! Elèna! Elèna!

FAUST.
Viandante languido
T'appressa al margine—

PAN. Canta.

ELENA.
Del flutto flebile.
Debile cantico t'invita, è

PAN. Canta.

ELENA.
Florida la via di mammole.
Cantan le tenere syrene, ecc., ecc.
(ELENA, PANTALIS escono.)

FAUST.
Elèna! Elèna! ecc.. ecc.

MEF. (*Entrando.* FAUST *si desta.*)
Ecco la notte del classico Sabba,
Gran ventura per te che cerchi vita
Nel regno delle favole;
Nel regno delle favole tu sei.
Saggio consiglio:
E di spiar ciascun nostra fortuna
Per opposto sentier.

HELEN.
Motionless floating, the moon floods the dome of [night—

PANTALIS. Sing on.

HELEN.
With rays of pallid light.

PAN.
Odors balsamic the boughs from the dews distill.

HELEN. Sing on.

PAN.
And all the warm air fill.

HELEN.
Goldfish and Sylphides light,
Nereids and cygnets white—

PAN. Sing on.

HELEN.
Swim on the reedy stream.
Softly the winds blow,

PAN. Sing on.

HELEN.
Full is the moon now,
Sing on, O Syren, thy serenade low.!

PAN.
Sing on, O Syren—sing on!

FAUST, (*Dozing.*)
Helena, Helena, Helena, Helena!

HELEN.
Move we now languidly,
Nearing the tranquil shore,

PAN. Sing on.

HELEN.
Whose waves moan evermore!
Faintly the spirit song woos thee still,

PAN. Sing on.

HELEN.
Flowers, fair and fragrant, the pathways fill.
Sweetly the Syrens are singing, etc.
(They go out.)

FAUST. (*Still on bank.*)
Helena, Helena, Helena, Helena!

MEF. (*Entering with* FAUST.)
This is the night of the classical Sabbath,
Good fortune 'tis for you, for new life seeking
In some old land of fables still;
In one old land of fable you now stand!
Now hear my counsel:
'Tis that we hence depart, each seeking fortune
On a different path.

FAUST.

Delibo l'aura del suo vago,
Idioma cantatrice!
Son sul suolo di Grecia!
Ogni mia fibra! é posseduta dall' amor. [*Escono.*

MEF.

Al Bròcken, fra le streghe del Nord,
Ben Io sapevo farmi obbedir.
Ma qui fra stranie larve più me stesso non trovo.
Atri vapori dell' irto Harz,
Acri catrami e resine!
O prediletti alle mie nari!
Un' orma di voi non fiuto in quest attica terra.
Ma qual s'inoltra volante o danzante
Gajetto sciame femminil? Vediamo!

(*Entrano le Coretidi. Danza in cerchi* MEFISTOFLE *annoiato e confuso esce.*) (*Entra* ELENA.)

CORETIDI. (*Cantando con varie pose in tuono dorico.*)

Ah! Trionfi ad Elèna carmini, corone,
Danze patetiche
Ludi di cetera.
Circonfu sa di sol il magico viso,
Tu irradi l'anime, riverberi il cielo.

ELENA. (*Assorta in una fatale visione*).

Notte cupa, truce, senza fine funèbre
Orrida notte d'Illio!
Implacato rimorso!
Nugoli d'arsa polvere al vento
Sur gono e fano più cieca la tenèbra.

CORETIDI. Pace!

ELENA.

Di cozzantisi scudi
E di carri stroscianti
E di catapulte sonanti
L'etere è scossa!
Si muta il suol in volutàbro di sanque.

COR. Numi! Numi!

ELENA.

I numi terribili già ruggono,
l'ire inferocendo della pugna;
L' ispide torri ergonsi tragiche, negre;
Fra la caligin densa.

COR. Elena!

ELENA.

L' incendio già lambe le case.
Veggonsi l' ombre degli
Achèi projette (bui profili giganti)
Vagolar le pareti in mezzo ai roghi.
Ahimè! ah! Alto silenzio regna poscia
Dove fu Troja.

(*Entra* FAUST *splendidamente vestito coll' abito dei Cavalieri del XV. secolo; e seguito da* MEF., NEREO, PANTALIS, *da piccoli Fauni e da Sirene.*)

CORO.

Chi vien? O strana, o mirabile vista!
Un ero tutto splendido s'inoltra.
Sul suo viso mestissimo si legge: Amor!
Volgiti Regina! Regina, volgiti e guarda.

FAUST.

I breathe the perfume of her idiom,
So tender, soft, and tuneful.
'Tis in Greece I am standing; [FAUST *retires*
My every fibre vibrates and tingles still with love.

MEF.

At Brocken, 'mong the hags of the North (*hoarsely*),
I knew the way to make all obey; [no longer.
But here 'mid these strange shadows I myself know
Terrific vapors of Rocky Hartz,
Bearing an odor resinous,
Ye are delicious to my nostrils! [culture.
A semblance of you I smell not in this land of high
But what approaches me, singing and dancing?
Is it a band of maidens fair? I'll see it!

(*Enter* CORETIDI, MEF. *annoyed and confused, retires.*

(HELEN *enters, followed by the Chorus.*)

CORETIDI.

Ah! Pæans to thee we raise, songs and garlands offer.
With dances passionate,
Her charms we celebrate, [tures,
'Neath the sun's radiant beams, thy beautiful fea-
Each spirit sad illume with heaven's bright reflection.

HELEN. (*Absorbed by a terrible vision.*) [ful,
Midnight darkness cometh, past compassion mourn-
Oh, horrid night of Illium!
Memory, dark and remorseful!
Volumes of ashes, stifling and hot, [more dark;
Impelled by the wind, make blinding shadows still

COR. Ah, peace!

HELEN.

And the rumbling of chariots,
With thunders from catapults mighty,
All the air is shocked. [slaughtered
The drenched soil floweth with the blood of the

COR. Save her, ye gods!

HELEN.

The gods in their dreadful wrath are thundering,
Urging all to frenzy for the battle; [looming,
Towers rough and sombre up thro' the shadows are
'Mid darkness overwhelming.

COR. Elena!

HELEN.

The fire's tongues of flame lick the houses.
Shadows of warriors then were seen,
Achaians (in their outlines gigantic) [reached us;
Walls are crashing around us, the flames have
Alas, ah! Desolate silence now is reigning
Where Troy enthroned was

(FAUST *enters, richly clad in the costume of a knight of the fifteenth century, followed by* MEF., NEREUS *and* PANTALIS, *with little fauns and sirens.*)

CHORUS.

Who comes? O strange and most wonderful vision
An illustrious hero is approaching.
On his features so pale and sad is written: I "love."
Turn you, sov'reign lady! Turn here, O queen, and behold him.

(FAUST. (*Inchinato davanti ad* ELENA.)

Forma ideal purissima
Della Bellezza eterna!
Un uom ti si prosterna
Innamorato al suol.
Volgi vêr me la cruna
Di tua pupilla bruna,
Vaga come la luna,
Ardente come il sole.
Un uom ti si prosterna, ecc.

ELENA.

Dal tuo respiro pendo e me chiamo beata

PAN.

Ah! quivi l'amor li aduna.

ELENA.

Ch' unica fra tutte le troadi e le argive ninfe
Spargo i voluttuosi fascini su cotanto amante!

FAUST.

La tranquillo immagine
Della fanciulla blanda
Ch' amai la fra le nebbie
D'una perduta landa
Già disvani,
Conquiso m' ha un piu sublime sguardo,
Un più fulgurato viso
E tremo ed ardo!
Adoro e tremo ed ardo!
Conquiso m'ha più sublime amor.
E adoro e tremo ed ardo, ecc.

MEF.

Oh, stupor! Prodigio!
Quivi l'amour liaduna!
Stupor! Stupor!
Guarda! Ah, qui li aduna l'amor!

CORO.

Quivi l'amor liaduna;
O stupor! Celeste coppia!
Sembran Endimione e Luna—
Celeste coppia! li aduna qui l'amor!

MEF.

Zitti lassù! Quivi l'amor, etc.

(MEFISTOFELE, PANTALIS, NEREO *e il* CORO *s'allontano.*)

FAUST. (*Kneeling before* HELEU.)

Form of ideal purity,
Beauty's eternal esence!
I kneel here in thy presence,
With loving adoration.
Upon me turn the tender gleaming
Of thy brown eyes beaming.
Like the morn, radiant seeming,
Sunlike, with ardor glowing.
Here, kneeling in thy presence, etc.

HELEN.

Over your sweet accents, happy am I still to linger.

PAN.

Ah, love, bring them here together!

HELEN.

How amid all these maidens, those lovely nymphs of Troy and Argos, [in words so tender?
Have my charms thus captur'd such love, express'd

FAUST.

Now the tranquil memories
Of that fair, pliant maiden,
I loved, in that lost region
Where skies with mists are laden,
Has disappeared; enslaved am I
By eyes with passion burning,
By beauty far more resplendent,
By charms transcendent!
Trembling, for love I am yearning—
Conquered by love far more sublime etc.

MEF.

Oh, amazing! Amazing!
Love brought them here together!
All 'mazed, all crazed! Look you?
Ah, they are here brought by love, etc.

CHORUS.

Love here brought them together!
All are 'mazed! Celestial couple!
Like Endymion and fair Luna!
Celestial couple, both hither led by love!

MEF.

Silence, you, there! Love brought them, etc.

(MEFISTOFELES PANTALIS, NEREUS *and* CHORUS *retire.*)

ELENA.

O incantesimo parla! quel magico soffio
Cotanto bèa là tua dolce loquela d'amore?
Il suon tu in serti al suon quasi
Alito d'eco d'estasi pieni.
Dimmi come farò a parlar bidioma soave?

FAUST.

Frugo nel cor e ti rispondo:

ELENA.

E mi rispondi: Ave!

FAUST.

Così tu pur come augello a richiamo,
Frughi nel cor e mi rispondi: t'amo!

ELENA.

T' amo! T'amo!

FAUST.

T'amo, t'amo, t'amo!

HELEN.

O enchanting words fill me!
Tell me, this magical cadence that so enhances
The charm of your amorous confession?
Tone sweetly follows tone like
The sound of an echo—full of emotion. [of loving?
Tell me how I may learn to speak that sweet idiom

FAUST.

I ask my heart that echoing answers—"loving!"

HELEN.

That echoing answers—"loving!"

FAUST.

As calls the bird to his mate, I would prove thee,
Ask of thy heart, and thus reply: "I love thee!"

HELEN.

I love thee—yes, I love thee!

FAUST.

I adore and love thee!

FAUST *e* ELENA.

Amore! misterio celeste, profondo!
Già il tempo dilegua, cancellasi il mondo!
Già l'ore dai tetri mortali contate
Ramingan serene per plaghe beate!

FAUST.

Amore!

ELENA.

E brividi ignoti mi cercan le vene—

FAUST *e* ELENA.

E'un aura dicantici esala il mio core.
Guardandoci inviso cantiamo l'amore,
Cantiamo l'amore.

FAUST.

Guardandoci inviso!

ELENA.

Cantiam amor!
Ah! l'amore, l'amore del'rio! l'amore sorriso.

FAUST.

Ah! l' amore visione.

FAUST *e* ELENE.

Ah! l'amore, cauzone, l'amore canzonesia
Sempre nel tardo futuro sommerso
Sia l'estre mo suo verso.
Ah! cantiamo l'amor—l'amor, mister, ecc.

BOTH.

This love is a mystery, profound and celestial.
Of time's flight forgetful, annulled are cares terres-
trial. [bered,
At last, when the hours of this earth-life are num-
We'll roam thro' fair regions by cares unencumber'd

FAUST.

Thus love is!

HELEN.

A tremor unknown thro' my veins now is stealing!

BOTH.

A breath too of poesy my heart is exhaling
On each other gazing, of love we are singing,
Of love ever singing.

FAUST

On each other gazing.

HELEN

We sing of love! [forever!
Ah, yes! love is a passionate fever, its smile lives

FAUST.

Ah, yes! love is a vision.

BOTH.

Ah! a poem Elysian, a blissful condition,
And be it hereafter, in mansions eternal,
Sung as the poem supernal;
We'll sing there of love, etc.

CORETIDI.

Poësia liberat'alza pe'cieli;
Voli di folgore! impeti d'aquila;
Spinganti all'ultime reggie del sol,
Alle reggie del sol. Si spinganti avol!
Ah! Ah!

ELENA.

Giace in Arcadia una placida valle—

FAUST.

Ivi insieme vivrem.

ELENA.

F. avrem per nido le grotte delle ninfe,
E per guanciale—

FAUST.

Le tue morbide chiome.

ELENA.

Ei fior del prato.

(Si perdono mormorando fra i cespugli.)

CORETIDI. Ah!

FINE DEL ATTO QUARTO.

CORETIDI.

Free as the eagle, song flies through the heavens,
Swift a thunderbolt, soaring so mightily
On to the ultimate realms of the sun,
And we sing of the sun. Yes! swift in its strong flight! Ah! Ah!

HELEN. *(Dreamily.)*

Down in Arcadia, lies a calm, placid valley.

FAUST. ((*Dreamily.*)

There together we'll live.

HELEN.

We'll have for shelter the grottos of the wood-nymphs.
And for a pillow—

FAUST.

Thy own soft, wavy tresses.

HELEN.

And meadow flowers.

(They disappear through the bowers.)

CORETIDI. *(Within the curtain.)* Ah!

END OF FOURTH ACT.

EPILOGUE.

THE DEATH OF FAUST.

FAUST.—Flying moments, stay; for thou art blissful!

SCENE—*Faust's labratory as in the First Act, but here and there delapitated by time. Magic voices in the air.* FAUST *meditates, seated in a large chair.* MEFISTOFELES *stands behind him like an incubus. Night. A lamp burns dimly. The Holy volume is open, as in Act I.*

FAUST.

O rimenbranza!

MEF. *(sotto voce con accenio sinistro fissando* FAUST.*)*

Cammina, cammina, superbo pensier,
La morte è vicina, cammina, cammina,
Superbo pensiero.

FAUST.

Corsi attraverso il mondo e i suoi mirraggi
Ghermii pel crine il desiderio alato!

MEF.

(O canti! o memorie d'incanti e di glorie,
Guidate a ruina quell' animo altier.)
Hai bramato, gioito
E poi bramato novellamente
Nè ancor dicesti all' attimo fuggente:
(Ironico.) Arrestati sei bello!

FAUST.

Ogni mortal mister gustai
Il Real, l' Ideale,
L'Amore della vergine,
L'Amore della Dea Si.
Ma il Real fu du dolore, e l'Ideal fusogno.

FAUST.

(Starting up, as if absorbed in an extatic vision.)

O power of mem'ry!

MEF.

(Softly gazing at FAUST *with evil expression.)*

Come onward, come onward, sublime is the tho't.
'Tis death now approaching, come onward,
Come onward: the thought is inspiring.

FAUST.

Thro'out the world, I've wander'd, its shams observing:
And catching passing fancies on the light wing.

MEF.

(O memories and stories of pleasure and of glories,
Lead on to utter ruin that spirit proud and high.)
You had longings, enjoyments,
And your longing soon found renewal.
You have not said to any flying moment;
(Ironically.) "Stay; thou art blissful!"

FAUST.

All mortal mysteries I have proved—
The Ideal, the Real;
The love of simple maidenhood,
And of the higher goddess—
Yet the Real was sorrow, and but a dream the Ideal

FAUST.

Giunto sol passo estremo
Della più estrema età
In un sogno supremo
Si bea l'anima già.
Re d'un placido mondo
D'una landa infinita a
Un popolo fecondo—
Voglio donar la vita.

MEF.

(Spiar voglio il suo cor.)

FAUST.

Sotto una savia legge
Vo' che surgano a mille,
A mille e genti e gregge
E case e campi e ville.

MEF.

(Ah! all' erta tentator.)

FAUST.

Ah! voglio che questo sogno
Sia la santa poesia
E l'ultimo bisogno
Dell' esistenza mia.
Ecco la nuova turba al guardo mio si svela!

MEF.

(Ah! qual baglior conturba
Il muto tenebror?)

FAUST.

Ecco il colle s'inurba e
Il popolo s'inciela.

MEF.

(Il bene gia gli si rivela!)

FAUST.

S'ode un cantico in ciel.

MEF.

(All'erta! All'erta! Tentator!)

FAUST.

Gia mi beo nell' augusto raggio
Di tanta aurora!
Gia nell' idea pregusto
L'alta ineffabil ora.

MEF.

(All'erta! All'erta!
E la battaglia incerta fra Satana ed il ciel.)

(A Faust, disciogliendo il mantello come nell' atto primo.)

Vedi! ch' io distendo il questo mantel
E volerem sull' aria!
Faust! Faust Faust!

FAUST.

Nearing the utmost limit
Of life's extremest goal,
In a vision delightful,
Did wander forth my soul.
King of some placid region,
Unknown to care and striving,
I found a faithful people—
And fain would aid their living.

MEF.

(Now I would read his heart!)

FAUST.

Under careful legislation,
I saw new towns arising—
A happy, pros'perous nation,
With homes and flocks surprising!

MEF.

(Ah! up tempter, do thy part!)

FAUST.

Ah! would then, that this fair vision
Could but be my last dream;
The latest earthly mission,
Of life's important scheme.
Look you! the crowds now come within my observation.

MEF.

(Ah! see—what gleam of light
Breaks on the silent night?)

FAUST.

Lo, the crowd turn t'wards cities—
Heavenward turns the nation.

MEF.

(Ah, 'tis from heaven a revelation!)

FAUST.

Holy songs now I hear—

MEF.

(Up, tempter! play your part.)

FAUST.

Now I bathe in the radiant splendor
Of heaven's glorious morning;
Ideal bliss upon my soul
Is already dawning!

MEF.

(Up tempter! thy part play.
'Twixt good and ill, the battle will here be fought to-day.)

(To Faust, arranging his cloak as in the First Act.)

Come. I have but to spread thus my cloak.
Swift thro' the air 'twill take us.
Faust! Faust! Faust!

FAUST. Cielo!

CORO.

Ah! Ave Signor! Signor de gli angeli,
Dei santi, delle sfere!

MEF.

(Esorcizzando verso l'alcova da dove appariscono le Sirene in mezzo ad una luce calda.)

Odi il canto d'amor
Che un di beò il tuo cor!
Vieni a inebbriar le vene
Sul sen delle sirene! Vieni!
[La visione delle Sirene s'oscura.

CORO. E dei santi Signor!
E dei volanti cherubini d'or!

FAUST. Arrestati sei bello!

MEF. (*Avventandosi verso* FAUST.)
Torci il guardo, torci il guardo!

FAUST.

(Con un gesto possente va ad afferrare il Vangelo.)

Baluardo m'e il Vangelo!

(Cadendo ginocchioni e appoggiandosi sulla Bibbia.)

MEF. Torci il guardo, torci il guardo!

FAUST.

Dio clementi m'allontana
Dal demonio mio beffardo;
Non indurmi in tentazione!
Vola il cantico ardente
Dell celestial drappello!
Sacro attimo fuggente,
Arrestati sei bello!
Ame l'eternità! *[Cade morto.*

MEF.

Strilla l'angelico stuolo,
Ghermiamo quell'anima al volo.
Gia l'opra del male destrugge Iddio
Col suo stolto perdon, col suo stolto perdon!

CORO. E dei volanti cherubini d'or!
Dall' eterna armonia
Dall'universo,
Nel glauco spazio immenso
Emana un verso di supremo amor.

(Scende una pioggia di rose sulla salma di FAUST.*)*

Spargiamo un profluvio, di rose,
Un nembo di foglie odorose,
Un effluvio di fior.
Oriamo la povera sulma s'invola
Redenta quell' alma nel mistico amor.

MEF. *(Sotto i raggi e sotto la pioggia di rose diabattendosi e irridendo.)*

Diluviam le rose sull' arsa mia testa
Le membra ho corrose dai raggie dai fior.
M'assale la mischia di mille, angioletti
Trionfan gli eletti ma il reprobo fischia! Eh!
Trionfa il Signor ma il reprobo fischia! ecc.

CHERUBINI.

Spargiamo un diluvio di rose sul mostro,
Le gelide e irose sue membra contorca,
Furente in mezzo alla pioggia rovente.
Alla pioggia rovente che spargono i cherubi d'oro.
Siam nimbi volanti dai limbi,
Nei santi splendori vagnati,
Nei santi splendor! Ave!

FAUST. Oh heaven!

CHORUS.

Ah! Hail sov'reign Lord of bright, angelic hosts.
And of all worlds created!

MEF.

(Throwing spells around the alcove where the sirens appear in a warm light.

Hear the sweet songs of love,
That your heart did so move;
Come, renew your emotion,
Thro' these nymphs of the ocean Come now.
[The sirens disappear

CHORUS. Thou of seraphs art Lord!
And of the cherubs with their wings of gold.

FAUST. (*with ecstacy*) Oh, stay thee, thou art blissful!

MEF. (*Approaching* FAUST.)
Turn your glances! Turn your glances!

FAUST.

(With a strong effort, he goes to fetch the Evangel.)

Here, at last, I find salvation,

(He falls kneeling on the sacred volume, and murmurs a prayer. The heavenly vision appears to him.)

MEF. Turn your glances! Turn your glances!

FAUST.

God of pity, save, O save me
From the snares that here enslave me!
Leave not to dire temptation
(*Carried away with ecstacy.*) Float around, loud Hosannas,
From hosts with heavenly banners!
Sacred moment fleeting,
Stay thee, stay thee, for thou art blissful!
To endless love I go! *[Dies.*

MEF.

Angels now wait for the dying;
His soul I will seize while 'tis flying.
The power of sin, that of goodness destroys,
With the pardon so stupid that mercy employs.

CHO. Lord of the cherubs with their gold wings,
From the harmonies eternal
Of wide creation—
From realms of space, wide extensive,
There rise loud anthems of supremest love.

(A shower of roses falls on FAUST'S *body.)*

We sprinkle a shower of roses
O'er him who in death now reposes,
Sweet odorous flowers.
We pray for the spirit that upward is soaring,
Redeem'd, forgiven thro' thy pard'ning love.

MEF. (*Under the brightness, and shower of roses, gradually sinks into the earth.*)

This deluge of roses upon my head falling,
My limbs have corroded and withered my powr's.
Assail'd thus by thousands of cherubs, no bliss is;
The saints may rejoice but the reprobate hisses. Eh!
The saints may rejoice but, etc.

CHERUBS.

A deluge of flow'rs o'er the monster we scatter,
His limbs thus corroding, his dread powers exploding,
His doom thus forboding.
Like raindrop's soft patter, our roses we scatter,
We cherubs with bright, golden pinions.
We're spirits from limbo upsoaring,
The regions celestial exploring,
The splendors above. All hail!